HUMANS WHO FEEL THINGS

BY KARLEE ROSE NORTH

karlee rose north

also by karlee rose:
permission to feel
permission to love
permission to be

contents
illustrations
and cover art by:
karlee rose

humans who feel things

*For my partner Aleyah,
who relentlessly reminds me
of how capable I am.*

(AND FOR MY INNER CHILD,
WHO NEVER GAVE UP ON US
EVEN AFTER ALL THESE YEARS
OF NEGLECT)
♡

karlee rose north

Copyright © 2023 by Karlee Rose North.
All rights reserved. No part of this publication may be reproduced, stored or transmitted in any form or by any means, electronic, mechanical, photocopying, recording, scanning, or otherwise without written permission from the publisher. It is illegal to copy this book, post it to a website, or distribute it by any other means without permission.

humans who feel things

FOR HUMANS WHO FEEL BIG EMOTIONS THAT THEY DON'T KNOW HOW TO PROCESS

karlee rose north

trigger warning

the contents of this book contain topics that may be heavy/triggering for some readers. these topics include:
depression

self-harm

sexual assault

please take care of yourself while reading.

united states sexual assault hotline **1-800-656-4673**
united states suicide prevention hotline **988**

additionally, the content in this book is intended for a mature audience. this book discusses sex explicitly and often. please do not read if you are not mature enough to digest the sexual content (notice how I didn't write an age, if you are a full-grown adult who is embarrassed by sexual content, please put this book down and do some introspection).

thank you. enjoy.

YOU DON'T HAVE TO HAVE EVERYTHING FIGURED OUT!

    HERE'S TO NOT KNOWING WHAT COMES NEXT, AND BEING ~~OKAY~~ ANYWAY.
                              CONTENT

karlee rose north

I wrote a book about vulnerability,
a book about love,
a book about chasing dreams,
and now I present to you,
a book about everything and nothing.
I hope you find something meaningful between
these pages

perhaps yourself?

a note from the author

hello sweet person holding my book. welcome to chaos. this is not your typical poetry book. she (yes I am gendering her), is a compilation of my thoughts, with no rhyme or reason. The biggest criticism I get online, is that my work is not "poetry". the poetry police survey my tik toks and alert me that I fail the test sometimes. and maybe what I write isn't all poetry (whatever that even means), but I like the idea of releasing expectations about what you think this should be. any of it: my words, this book, this silly little life. release. your. expectations. this is my (very public) diary. I have filled it with thoughts, poetry, prose, doodles, cursing. this is a deep dive inside the mind of a twenty-something queer person, trying to navigate the world and the people in it. I have not set out to make it my mission to be perfect. my mission is to be honest. to be vulnerable. the biggest thing that often holds writers back from publishing, are the gatekeeping publishers. and since I am able to self-publish (thanks amazon!), I can really do this thing however the hell I want. there are no editors breathing down my neck, tainting my authenticity with their expectations. and maybe someday I will sign a publishing deal, but I have really been enjoying this "self"-publishing thing. I get to do it all. every decision is mine to make, including the "contents" list in this book. the hardest thing about writing books for me is organizing all of my thoughts into categories (sections, chapters, etc.) it's too hard. I don't want to. so I quite literally am not going to. like I said, release your expectations of this book. and please return this book (amazon returns can be dropped off at any UPS store), if anything I've said so far has pissed you off. I better not get a one-star review because you had unfair expectations of what this book should be. so either open your mind or print your return label and get your $15 back. but if you are still here, I am so happy to have you. this is me. raw. vulnerable. authentic. me. these are things that run through my head, thoughts that fill my journals, and the doodles, well those are just for fun.

welcome to the HUMANS WHO FEEL THINGS series. this series is for humans (me and you), who feel things (every single one of us). the goal of this book is to validate all that you feel, and to wipe your tears/hold your hand while you feel them. write in this book, SCREAM INTO IT, run it over. do whatever you gotta do. take care of yourself throughout this process. ya know, the "feeling" process. it's not as easy as it sounds.

I love you so fucking much.

Kar

CONTENTS

I was going to divide this book into sections, but I have deemed it too stressful to categorize all of my feelings into organized chapters so you will just have to tolerate the emotional roller-coaster that is this book, and if you haven't read my work before, please brace yourself for lots of run-on sentences too, I have lots of thoughts and I don't always like to separate them. oops.

karlee rose north

HUMANS WHO FEEL THINGS

karlee rose north

what if everyone
stopped caring so much
about who I love,
          and started caring more
         about loving each other?
                  -you have twisted your
                "faith" into an untie-able
                          knot.

humans who feel things

I love women.

that's the poem.

karlee rose north

I find myself in the parts of her
that she doesn't like about herself
I find myself in the marks on her thighs
I find myself in the shape of her breasts.
I find myself in the curves of her body
I find myself in the arch of her back

In the parts of herself that
she finds hard to love,
I find myself.

humans who feel things

HATE SPEECH AND DIESEL TRUCKS

I let go of her hand
when we cross busy streets
because I still haven't decided
if losing my life
would be worth being free.
don't you see how much I love her?
doesn't our love light something in you?
who cares if we both have vaginas
who cares what our love means to you?
-I do.

THE LGBTQIA COMMUNITY, NOT THE CATHOLIC CHURCH

I've spent my entire life judging people like me
because I was taught that we are outsiders
that we don't belong
so I've spent forever judging them
and somehow,
they still let me in.

humans who feel things

if you are a human that feels things,
I am so sorry.
how much easier it is to feel numb.

karlee rose north

and I write and I write and I write
to try to make sense of it all
but I've written four books
and nothing makes much sense at all.

what is the point of it all? what is the point of it all? what is the point of it all? what is the point of it all? what is the point of it all? what is the point of it all? what is the point of it all? what is the point of it all? what is the point of it all? what is the point of it all? what is the point of it all? what is the point of it all?

humans who feel things

a poem about heartbreak

the hardest part about you being gone
isn't just the absence of your company.
it is doing the daily routine that became *ours*,
without *you*.

karlee rose north

I wish I knew you were
going to become a memory,
before you became one
I may have laughed a little harder
in your company
held you a little tighter
when you hugged me

if I knew our last moment together was
in fact, the last one we would ever have,

I would have spent more time
loving you
and less time wondering
what my week would look like

I would have spent more time listening
and less time talking

if I had only known…
but we never get to

and that's why you need to
tell them how much they mean to you
please, because one day,
will be the last one that you see them,
and after that you will only see them
in your memory.

humans who feel things

HOW IT FEELS TO GRADUATE

I have been feeling so aimless lately,
like my life has no meaning
tbh I haven't felt
purposeful since college
going to class gave me purpose
extracurriculars gave my life meaning
now I sit alone in my apartment
trying to find the words to explain
this emptiness
that consumes me
even love cannot fill the void
that the education system
has left in me.
I crave the validation
that comes from
the good grades and feedback
without it
I feel empty
I have been a shell of myself since graduation
desperately trying to figure out what else can fill
me.

karlee rose north

I crave the feeling of being in control
    (coping mechanism for not feeling like I had any as a child)

humans who feel things

in college,
I so desperately craved male attention
I would think to myself,
"could he be the *one*?"
whenever I met someone new.
after freshman year,
I thought,
"it is time to kick it up a gear"
so I lost weight and put on more makeup
and yet,
the only attention I got was
from the drunk dudes at frat parties.
senior year rolled around
and I still didn't have a boyfriend.
and that's when I realized
that it wasn't the boys I was trying to find,
it was myself.

-the tale of the closeted college kid

karlee rose north

the female body
is a wonderland to explore
you better take your time
and make her feel good
or she will devour you
in her beauty.

humans who feel things

when she holds me
I feel safer
than I ever have.
when she touches me
I feel more alive
than I ever have.
when she looks at me
I know that I have
found a home
in her eyes.

karlee rose north

I run my finger across her skin
and her body rises to me
like I am the only god
it believes in.

humans who feel things

IF WOMEN WERE ONLY ~~MENT~~ MEANT TO BE WITH MEN, THEN WHY DO I, AS A WOMAN, LOVE BOOBIES SO MUCH?

karlee rose north

our love is so powerful
it consumes me
and heals me
and releases me
a better version than before.

humans who feel things

my heart aches for you,
even when we are together
because it already knows
that it will shatter if you leave.

they say your first love never lasts
how devastated I will be if that's true

karlee rose north

why have I been feeling so numb?
where has all of the feeling gone?
I haven't been feeling like myself,
and I don't know where it is
I have gone
I feel numbness
I feel hopeless
I crave to feel
just an ounce of hope
just an ounce of joy

humans who feel things

I have started leaning on shopping to cope
with all of the numbness I feel
buying something new
gives me a sliver of bliss
that is until my credit card payment is due
and then I remember that the joy
wasn't really true
it was a temporary fix
for this deep void

fuck.

karlee rose north

m e n t a l   h e a l t h

what does it mean?
 how do I help my mind
when it forces me to run and hide
 my problems, they eat me alive
and my mind just forces me to numb
 and stay inside
and binge tv
 and remove myself from reality.

humans who feel things

what happens if I believe in myself?

karlee rose north

I have found my purpose,
and it is to write
and to share
and to connect
and to buy a house in Maine
and open the windows
and breathe in fresh air
and bask in sunlight
and write books
and sell my art
and be a full time creative

that is my purpose
I have so much clarity about it

I just don't know how to get there
when I feel stuck h e r e.

humans who feel things

the last time I walked
barefoot in the grass
it was so plush and
green and divine
the sky was so blue
and the air held the warmth
of a summer day in maine
with each footstep
I felt the earth running up
through my veins
the laughter of my friends
filled the air
along with left over
pad thai and hard cider

karlee rose north

I thought that this was the life I wanted
a beautiful new apartment in a quiet area
where I could go on runs and ride my bike
but what I really want is to go back up north
where the summer breeze is refreshing
and the streams whisper sweet melodies
florida has given me a home
and I am so grateful for that
but my time here has expired
mother nature is calling me
I need to go.

humans who feel things

dear body,
we have been through a lot together,
haven't we?
god, I used to hate you so much,
but somehow, you never hated me.
you held me when my world fell apart
and you held me when we felt on top of it.
you never gave up on me when I starved you
and you never gave up on me
when I pushed you to your limits.
everyone has always told me
that you are beautiful,
I'm sorry it has taken me so long to believe it

dear body,
this is my apology letter to you
I'm so sorry I didn't write it sooner.

karlee rose north

dear stranger,
my wish for you,
is that you always prioritize joy.
I hope you never settle for less than you deserve
and I hope you know exactly what that means
for you.
I hope when you are invited to spend your day
by the lake or the ocean
that you never turn down the opportunity.
I hope you spend enough time resting,
life can be so hard sometimes.
I hope that you never run from opportunities
especially, if it's the opportunity to fall in love
I really hope you fall in love.
but more importantly, I hope you love your life.
I hope you wake up every day
with curiosity and excitement seeping
from your pores.
I hope you live a life that never bores you.
I hope you create the life of your dreams for
yourself.
because my dear stranger,
you deserve all that you want out of this life.
get out there and take it.

humans who feel things

I used to run from vulnerability,
now we dance in the space between
my paper and pen.

karlee rose north

your fingers slide
up the side of my neck
and wrap themselves around it
and squeeze me
until I lose my breath
and then you release me and
I catch my breath
and you slip your fingers
inside of me
and I lose it all over again.

humans who feel things

        push me
pull me
        touch me
f u c k
        me…

        but do it
s l o w l y
        so it never ends.

karlee rose north

it is so hard for me to write
about queer sex…
pussy-licking
and *fingering*
and the *female orgasm*
we were conditioned to believe
that these things are so dirty
so *wrong*…
but I know for a fact
        when she makes me arch my back,
                our love feels so *right*…

humans who feel things

WHAT'S THE BIG DEAL?

I didn't know that sex could be comfortable
    until her
I knew the experiences I had were
    not sex
        but I wanted them to be
            so badly...
because everyone was losing their virginities
and I was 19 and feeling like
    I got left behind.

humans who feel things

we are taught to feel guilty
about having sex.
and we are taught to feel guilty
about being queer.
so imagine how we all feel
about queer sex!

karlee rose north

when I was 6 years old
a girl told me to touch her
under the sheets of the pull-out couch
she told me it would feel good...
it didn't.
she told me "everyone does it"
I didn't believe that other 6-year-olds did it.
our parents walked out
and caught us under the sheets
of the pull-out couch.
and that was the last time I saw the girl
who molested me when I was 6.

humans who feel things

you never know
you are experiencing trauma
when you are young
you don't always understand
why you feel so funny
you don't understand
why they make you feel so sad
until you are 18
and you realize that you were
sexually assaulted by a girl
who was supposed to be your friend.

karlee rose north

I crave you
like the ocean
craves the breeze
like the forest
craves the trees
my bones ache for you
when we are apart
like you are the very thing
that holds them together.

humans who feel things

I feel suffocated by comparison.
it has it's claws around my neck.
and I can't breathe.
I can't think.
I can't live.
I can't be.
I see how everyone else
lives their lives,
and I have no
fucking idea
how to live mine.

karlee rose north

<u>xmas list:</u>

-quiet time inside of my mind
-a little gay kiss
-thoughts that feel like mine
-moisturizer
-to learn how to love myself
-a vibrator

humans who feel things

it is not my job to be digestible.

karlee rose north

TODAY

today the crisp november air
takes me back to upstate new york
the breeze carries me and the trees
through the pages of memories
the magic of my hometown
finds me here
in this crispy november breeze

humans who feel things

isn't it magical
how a sip of sugar cookie latte
can take me back to a place
that no longer exists

isn't it magical
how i can exist in that place
that place that only lives
in my memories now
with people
who no longer know me
and roads that no longer
lead to places
i need to be

is my heart the one that has frozen over?
I sit across from a man who sings at his table. I am doing work on my laptop, his voice is soft and not particularly bothersome. But my reaction is to shame him. to make him stop. and all i do is simply notice these feelings arise in me. earlier i passed a woman in the bathroom who didn't smile at me. and i thought it was rude. but i often don't smile at the strangers that I pass. I think to myself that human kindness has disintegrated in this world. but more importantly, i think human kindness has disintegrated in me. so i listen to the man singing next to me and admire his joy. i pass the strangers in the bathroom and give them the smile that *i need.*

humans who feel things

HOMESICK

today i woke up feeling homesick
my body ached for the way the light shines into
the dining room of my childhood home
my skin craved the chilly fall mornings and the
feeling of warmth that washes over me when i
drive familiar roads
my heart craved the feeling of hugging my loved
ones, and having dinner with them more often
than a few times a year
sometimes i think moving so far away
was a mistake
i have already spent the majority of the time we
will ever have together, if i never move back to
the valley,
where everyone in my family will live out the
rest of their days

i'm not sure if i miss the town
or the person i was when i lived there

KINGSTON, NY

does my heart long for kingston, ny?
or does it long for snowy mornings?
and familiar chatter?
do i miss my hometown?
or do i miss the bagel shop?
or the inn on the corner?
do i miss ny?
or do i miss walks with my mother?
or drives with my brother?
do i miss it?
or do I miss the details?
the apple picking?
warm cider?
empty malls?
stops signs?
red lights?
the slowness of it all?

humans who feel things

HOMETOWN

their faces look older
their laughter sounds the same
the places and faces and smells
take me right back
to 2017
the year i left this place
but when i step off the plane
it all feels the same

karlee rose north

sometimes I dream of you
holding me
comforting me
and then I reach up
to grab your cheek
and you disappear
and I remember that
I am only dreaming
and that you
are no longer here.

(losing my grandmother (nanny) was the
greatest loss of my life, I think. I don't think
anything has ever hurt the way that did)

humans who feel things

the story of how we fell in love
starts with a few drunken nights
filled with flirting and spooning
that our sober minds convinced us was harmless
and then she infiltrated my thoughts
and the thought of her lips on mine
consumed me
i was consumed by the yearning
i had for her
my mind craved her
my body craved her
and night after night we would drink and flirt
and i would resist the burning desire she lit
inside

FOR A LONG TIME, I LOOKED
FOR ANSWERS IN THE BOTTOM OF
THE GLASS.

        ALL I EVER FOUND WAS
        EMPTINESS AND A HEADACHE

humans who feel things

ROLE MODEL

my mother raised two children on her own.
I was 3, my brother was a newborn
she found my hands covered in cocaine
she found my baby brother
covered in his own poop
and she made the hardest decision of her life,
(to leave the man she loved)
to give us a good one.
she worked the longest hours and gave us the
life that we deserved.
she married the man that we needed in our lives,
and he gave us a new family.
I got a sister, and another brother
and a man who never
expected me to call him *dad*
I didn't have a "perfect" childhood,
but I was always loved
I was always nourished
I was always safe

my mother did the best she could
with what she had
and that's all I could ever ask of myself too:
to do my best
with what I have
to make it work
to survive

I love you mom.

I dream of a life filled with love + laughter
I dream of a life that I am already living
all that's left is to recognize that.
    this <u>is</u> the life of my dreams

humans who feel things

is love not just offering your last piece of gum?

karlee rose north

there are so many versions of my life
I'm not sure which direction to go in.

humans who feel things

what if I fail?
what if I don't?

karlee rose north

I was the golden child, athlete, honor roll student
and now I'm the queer, fat, waitress
that nobody brings up anymore.

humans who feel things

are you still proud of me are you still proud of me are you still proud of me are you still proud of me are you still proud of me are you still proud of me are you still proud of me are you still proud of me are you still proud of me are you still proud of me are you still proud of me

karlee rose north

I have a huge mess of feelings swirling around in my head and I can't get the tornado to stop spinning long enough to see what's causing the storm.

humans who feel things

maybe my words will save the world.
or maybe they might save you.
and that's far more than I could've
ever asked them to do.

karlee rose north

WHAT ITS LIKE BEING A WOMAN

i look over my shoulder
at the men walking behind me
and i wonder if they are
going to try to rape me

humans who feel things

i know my brother has never
looked over his shoulder
and worried
about the things that
my mother told me to worry about
i know he only looks ahead

karlee rose north

I've been feeling big emotions since
 I was a kid
  I never understood what they meant
  or what I should do with them
   but now I understand that
   they have been my guides all along.
    Showing me the way.

humans who feel things

<u>how to create when you are depressed:</u>
-don't
-can't
-won't
-write a 7-page rant about capitalism
and feeling heartbroken for the versions
of you that no longer exist.

for a long time I thought being with a man was my only option. and when I never felt any attraction toward them in college, I thought something was wrong with me. but then I started to actually feel something. something that felt so good and natural. something that I expected to feel towards a man. but the feelings were for a woman. and that is when i started to realize, that being queer isn't a choice (like society was trying to condition me to believe). because I did not choose to fall in love with a woman. that is not the easier choice. i would have chosen a man if i could have. but that is not how sexuality works. as a queer woman, all i ask is that you stop trying to tell me that what i feel is wrong. because i can fucking promise, that i spent years trying to make my feelings go away. I couldn't. we can't. we won't.

we love to be happy and in love just like you do.

humans who feel things

i don't *need* the external validation
but it is nice sometimes.

karlee rose north

you are allowed
to change.

nothing in nature
ever stays exactly
the same

humans who feel things

A PRAYER

hail mary
full of grace
the lord is with thee
blessed art thou who love women
and blessed is the fruit between her thighs
holy woman
lover of goddesses
give in to your sins
now and at the hour of your death.
amen.

things I've learned since coming out:

- people who "don't support your lifestyle" do not deserve your love.

- my sexuality is not just a "lifestyle", it's a part of me. and it will forever affect the way that the world treats me.

- I am capable of deep love and vulnerability.

- queer friends have been an integral part of my self-acceptance.

- I will never stop having to come out to people, but there is nothing wrong with keeping my sexuality to myself if I don't feel safe.

- queer love is magic.

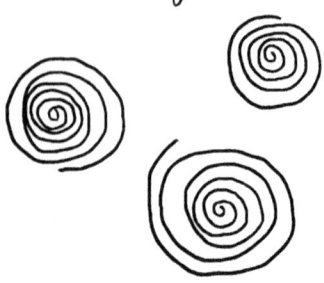

humans who feel things

<u>is this real life?</u>

i think to myself as I feel overwhelmed with gratitude. the car that I drive, the person i wake up next to when i open my eyes. this beautiful day and beautiful run by the bay. i am overwhelmed with gratitude as i breathe deep and soak up the sun's rays on my skin. is this real life? because sometimes it's more beautiful than i could've ever imagined.

karlee rose north

perhaps life is about
nothing at all
perhaps?
perhaps?
perhaps?

humans who feel things

i have always put so much time and energy into dreaming of somewhere else, that i've spent way too long not appreciating where i am. you see, you can't wait until you can run a marathon to be happy. you can't wait until you weigh some arbitrary "goal" weight to be satisfied. you can't plan for a future and save your happiness for it. you need to be happy and satisfied and pack your days full of joy. soak it all up. i promise you there will still be some for when you accomplish your goals but the true joy: the true magic, comes from the smaller wins. the little moments. the ones so delicate and small that they are far too often missed. look for those. and let those sweet little magical moments become your life.

karlee rose north

i went for a run on the trail today
and everyone who passed me
had earbuds in their ears
they were listening to art
and without the vulnerability
of artists who create:
music, podcasts, audiobooks,
their runs would be shit
their workout would be boring
they would be miserable
art recharges us in an inexplicable way
but society still shits on the artist for "dreaming"
well dreams come true
next time you open a book
or turn on the radio
remember the creator of that art
and be careful how you talk about
the pursuit of art not being a "career",
because you need art
i need art
we all do
it makes the mundane tolerable
elevates the good times
and holds us through the bad times
so
show some goddman *respect.*

humans who feel things

how do I stop comparing myself to others?
how do I stop comparing my life to theirs?
how do I stop wanting what they have?
how? how? how?

karlee rose north

sometimes I grab my journal
when I'm hurting.
sometimes I grab my journal
when I'm happy.
but I always need it most
when I'm *numb*.

humans who feel things

Writing as a career path is similar to marrying a woman: they might not understand it, but they are not the one's feeling what I feel.

karlee rose north

don't feel so bad about blaming other people for things, sometimes it really is ~~theirs~~ fault.
　　　　　　　their

humans who feel things

sometimes I think getting a tattoo
will change my life.
sometimes I think getting
new shoes will too.
sometimes I think moving
across the country will save me.
maybe it would.
but it probably wouldn't

karlee rose north

what do I know about the world
and how it works?

what do I know about a heart
and how it hurts?

maybe rain and pain are born
in the same place.

humans who feel things

I always think I will be happier
down the road.
but here I am
with fresh tattoos
and expensive new shoes
and still no clue who I am.

karlee rose north

you said you
LOVE eating
me out...
I have never felt so
divine in my life.

I am your delicacy
and you are
mine.

humans who feel things

I'm proud of you for ~~being vulnerable~~ having no fucking clue what you are doing, but showing up and doing it anyway.

karlee rose north

I used to only write about
trauma and sadness
but now that I know love,
I write about trauma and sadness
and love.

humans who feel things

SOMETIMES WE MUST DO HARD BUT NECCESARY THINGS.

karlee rose north

you are on top of me,
we are elevated by our energy
it flows back and forth between us
pleasure shoots through my veins
you bite my neck
my head falls back
euphoria fills my mind

-I could get used to this

humans who feel things

I thought being in a relationship
would feel different than it does.
it doesn't feel like something I am a part of,
it just feels like something that I am.
she feels like an extension of myself.

karlee rose north

how do we slow down
in this fast-paced world?
when I start to pump the
breaks and take it slow,
I am nearly run off the road
by pressures and expectations
and rules and questions
"where are you going?"
"what are you doing?"

I'm slowing down
figuring out who it is
that I want to be,
who it is that I am.

humans who feel things

I am happy
until I'm not
I am sad
until I'm not
I am angry
until I'm not
I am hopeful
until I'm not
I am frustrated
until I'm not

we are here
until we're not

emotions are just as fleeting
as we are.

karlee rose north

slowing down is hard
but important.

humans who feel things

moans are the sounds
that my heart makes
when she feels good
and I never hold her back
because she has spent so long
being silenced by me...
she demands to be heard

karlee rose north

KISS WHOEVER YOU WANT,

PRIORITIZE EXPLORATION
AND JOY.

humans who feel things

Sometimes love looks like
deep conversations during
long car rides
    and other times
   it looks like deep dives
         between her thighs

karlee rose north

my back arches for you
my pulse quickens for you
my pussy pulsates for you

-my body knew it wanted you before
my mind had the chance to disagree.

humans who feel things

do I love my life?
does it love me?

karlee rose north

a wet pussy is an ocean
waiting to be explored
ignore her,
and she will drown you
in her desperation.

humans who feel things

when I feel grief,
I always feel you.
I always see you.
I always hear you.
when I think of grief,
it's always you.
       you.
              you.
                     you.
you taught me what it
feels like to
lose a piece of myself
forever.

karlee rose north

you can grow out of
people too.

humans who feel things

breathe in,
　　　breathe out.

things work out for you.
　　　　I promise.

writers block

i throw words together
like the clothes onto my closet floor
hoping to put something nice together
but i just keep making a mess

i don't know where my inspiration is hiding
i look for it in the sunsets and rolling clouds
i ask for her between each of my breaths
and she never answers
she is never seen
i miss her so much

how do i give advice about a life that i don't
understand?

humans who feel things

THINGS I'D LIKE MY 12 YEAR OLD SELF TO KNOW (FROM 24 YEAR OLD ME)

1. stop starving yourself for the attention of boys that will never love you.
2. stop worrying so much about dad's sobriety. (he'll be okay, you'll be okay too)
3. It gets easier to live without Nan.
4. you are so incredibly beautiful!
5. stop seeking validation from the people in your life. (you'll never get it)
6. always try to be your own biggest fan. (I'll forever be yours)
7. keep writing and making art! (you're really good at it)
8. do more things that make you smile.
9. your body is beautiful! the number on the scale cannot ever change that.
10. I know acne is embarrassing but stop stressing! (it clears up ☺)
11. nothing lasts forever (esspecially pain)
12. always make time for friends + your siblings (their pretty cool) actually

♡

karlee rose north

maybe i need to start
writing songs that will never be sung
maybe those will be good poems

humans who feel things

you tell me vs. show me poem

you tell me i'm so beautiful
and then you show me that i'm flawed
you tell me that i'm intelligent
and then you show me that
i don't know anything
you tell me that you are so proud of me
and then you show me that there are more
successful people in this world
you tell me sweet things
and show me ugly truths
i wish you would just show me what you tell me
and stop leaving me so confused

karlee rose north

when i was 16 i was told that a man would never
be attracted to the markings on my inner thighs

when i was 22 a women kissed them and
admired their beauty

humans who feel things

I told him it wasn't gonna happen,
but he begged me to let him have a taste.

he went down on me, I went down on him.

I washed him out of my mouth,
he washed me out of his.

I dropped him off at the bus stop,
then deleted his number.

karlee rose north

GOOGLE SEARCH HISTORY

Q IS IT RAPE IF I DIDN'T SAY NO?

Q how do I know if I have feelings for my best friend?

Q what does love feel like?

Q How do I know if I'm a lesbian?

?

humans who feel things

she opens her legs
he dives in
and sucks the life
out of her

karlee rose north

COMPARISON KILLS

I want to be happy with what I've got
but all I ever notice is all that
I am not.

humans who feel things

this isn't ~~the~~ the end
 of your story,
  it's only the beginning.

karlee rose north

I want to be everywhere and nowhere at all times.

humans who feel things

am I on your mind?
as much as you're on mine?
do you think of me?
as much as I think of you?

maybe we are all looking
for something that doesn't exis[t]
but maybe,
just maybe,
it doe[s]

— hope

♡

humans who feel things

you have permission to be afraid
of what comes next.
      you are allowed to not have
      a plan. you are allowed to
      <u>make peace with it</u>.

karlee rose north

SOMEDAY YOU'LL ~~WILL~~
REALIZE THAT
NONE OF IT MATTERED.

humans who feel things

THERE
　　IS
　　　　NOTHING
　　　　　　WRONG
　　　　　　　　WITH
　　　　　　　　　　YOU.

karlee rose north

TO THE GIRL WHO WROTE ME A BAD REVIEW ON AMAZON

maybe I'm not a "good" writer,
but I will keep writing my heart out
until the day that it stops beating.
so there's that I guess.

★★★★★

humans who feel things

I want to take a trip inside my mind
with a notebook and a glass of wine
I will jot field notes
about the things I find
I want to take a trip inside my mind

karlee rose north

SOLIDARITY

when you tell me that
my writing saved you,
I need you to know,
that my writing is the only thing
that saved me too.

humans who feel things

I ask people questions abaut their food all day,
    I ask myself questions abaut my life all night.

Guest Check: WHAT DO I WANT!?

DO WE EVER FIGURE OUT WHAT WE WANT TO BE WHEN WE GROW UP.

humans who feel things

my words beg me to share them
with you.

"your too sensitive"

is such a silly thing to say to me
because I tend to feel nothing at all
most times.

humans who feel things

THE "FEELINGS" GAME

I take a sip
it feels like euphoria
I take two more
I forget what it feels like to feel
and then there I am
passed out on the floor.

karlee rose north

I don't think my mother is always happy for me
I think she might be jealous of the parts of me
that she will never be.

humans who feel things

blue jeans
skin tight
sucked in
feels right
curvy hips
thick thighs
zipped up
tucked in
mission
accomplished.

karlee rose north

seasons remind me
that it's okay to let go
              to rest
              to grow
              to play

humans who feel things

THE FAT GIRL WHO ALWAYS HAD SOMETHING TO PROVE

i had to push myself so much harder to show
them that i could keep up
my inner motivation is crazy high because
that little fat girl is still inside
i had to prove that i was more than the
stereotype
that i was funny, strong, kind, intelligent
i worked so hard to make sure that the only way
people described me wasn't just "fat girl"
i don't know how to listen to my body
because she has always been my worst enemy
my body has never looked the same
as my teammates
as my friends
as the characters in my favorite tv shows
and so I learned to hate her
I've been chasing a different body
since the very day I learned how

karlee rose north

A RANT ABOUT GROWING UP FAT

I HATE GOING TO THE DOCTOR BECAUSE THEY WILL ALWAYS WEIGH ME AND ALWAYS DO THAT SIGH BEFORE THEY TELL ME ABOUT A HEALTHY BMI AND HOW I NEED TO LOSE WEIGHT BUT OTHERWISE I AM TOTALLY HEALTHY AND MY BLOOD LOOKS NORMAL AND EVERYTHING IS GREAT EXCEPT FOR THE FACT THAT I AM TOO FAT.

anyway so now I'm 24 and I haven't had a primary care doctor since I was 18 because they will tell me that I'm fat and totally disregard anything I say about how I feel or what I do for my health because how could I possibly be fat and healthy?

humans who feel things

betrayal is the burning sensation in the back of your head after you accidentally breathe in pool water.

karlee rose north

I have always been told
who to be.
I have always been
reminded of what the world
expects from me.
I have always been a robot
in this system.

but I've escaped now,
and it's scary here,
but exillerating.

                    AM I FREE?

humans who feel things

my writing career started as a 9 year old
with a value pack of gel pens from Sam's Club,
and a dream to share my words with the world.
it started with the stories I wrote in Microsoft Word
during my 45 minute slot on the family computer
each night. my career started with a dream,
one that I've ~~kept~~ kept hidden my entire life,
until a global pandemic forced the world around me
to slow down, and in return, forced my inner world
to break open, revealing magic and creativity
that I hadn't known since my childhood. so I
traded my lab coat for the empty page, and I
never looked back.

                             - about me

karlee rose north

do we know who we are at our core?
do we know what lights us up,
what tears us down?
I'm not sure that I do.
I'm not sure that anyone does.
are we all just reflections of each other?
the result of blending in too hard?
I don't know who I am
without every person I've ever known.

humans who feel things

repeat after me:

I set healthy boundaries with the people I love,
because I love and respect myself.

karlee rose north

the room is spinning
I'm blacking out
he pulls me in
we're making out
I can't feel a thing
but I know he is slipping
his fingers up my skirt
the room is spinning.

humans who feel things

I used to get drunk at frat parties
and make out with boys
that I would never see (or recognize)
ever again
just so I would know
that you weren't the last lips
that mine kissed.

humans who feel things

I spent my college years
taking shots and passing tests
and secretly coming to terms
with the fact that I had
fallen in love
with my best friend.

karlee rose north

sometimes we grow out of people,
the same way our pants don't fit
our shirts feel too tight
and our coats no longer zip
as easily as they used to.

humans who feel things

I believe that people
are meant for seasons
of your life,
and when the
next season comes,
it's okay to let them go.

karlee rose north

a thank you letter to the strangers that unknowingly changed my life

to the solo female hiker that
calmed my debilitating anxiety
to the solo female runner
who encouraged me to face my fears
to the solo females everywhere
that have inspired me out of
my comfort zone,
this is a thank you letter

being you
saved me
thank you, endlessly.

humans who feel things

I get to write for a living now, and two years ago
I was filling out medical school applications.

I get to spend the rest of my life with my best
friend, and two years ago, I was fantasizing
about a reality in which she were mine.

life is wild.

karlee rose north

for the first time in my entire life,
I feel like I am exactly where I need to be.

humans who feel things

the love of my life
came out of nowhere
it's funny to think
about all of the times
I was told love finds you
when you least expect it
because it does

and it did.

karlee rose north

queer love is magic ✧✦

humans who feel things

I slip my fingers
between my thighs
as I think of you.
I feel myself cum alive
as I think of you.
         you.
                 you.

karlee rose north

she pulls my hair
    as I arch my back
    and she slips inside
        my face is in the pillow
        her hands are gripping my waist
            -doin' it from behind

humans who feel things

I never thought I was a romantic
that was until you showed me
what it feels like to be someone's
first thought.

-no longer an after thought

karlee rose north

I always thought I'd marry a man,
and that's because that is all everyone
had ever said I'd do
I was born to be a wife
raised to be a mom.
when I fell in love with a woman,
I realized maybe I was always meant
to be those things,
but it was never supposed to be a man
that I'd be with.
maybe we should be teaching little girls
to fall in love,
not just give birth
maybe they should learn how
to process their emotions
before they learn how to open a condom
maybe they should be encouraged to
explore their own bodies
before they let anyone else explore theirs
we are teaching little girls
the wrong things

humans who feel things

i'm so deeply emotional,
I leave parts of myself everywhere I go

why are deeply emotional people the bad guys
when all we have ever wanted is to feel
u n d e r s t o o d.

karlee rose north

I AM SO DEEPLY EMOTIONAL, HOW COOL!

:)

humans who feel things

reader,

thank you endlessly for reading my words.
I hope that you have found some comfort in them, as
I have found comfort in sharing them with you. as
always, take care of yourself, and never hesitate to
reach out if you need someone to talk to.

I love you,

karlee rose

karlee rose north

about the author

karlee rose is a twenty-four-year-old queer poet looking to connect to the world with her poems, prose, and thoughts. she has been writing poems since she was a little girl and has been enjoying the bliss of sharing them. she has a science degree she probably won't ever use. so for now, she shares her words with you. the ultimate goal of her poetry is to be a safe haven for the queer community, as well as bring representation to the poetry world: especially in regard to queer love, sex, and intimacy.

you can find her on
tik tok @karleenorth
and
Instagram @karleerosenorth

Printed in Great Britain
by Amazon